FROM BREAKING THROUGH PIGEONHOLES TO LIVING LIFE BY DESIGN

FROM BREAKING THROUGH PIGEONHOLES TO LIVING LIFE BY DESIGN

Staci A. Imamura

This book is dedicated to everyone who has been an influence on who I am today! Thank you for all of the impactful conversations, the lessons and the motivation. May those interactions, as well as this book, have as strong of an impact on you as you have on me!

Please continue to impact the world in your own unique way!

Staci A. Imamura

ISBN: 978-0-578-57651-0

TABLE OF CONTENTS

FOREWORD

I first met Staci in June of 2013 at a Personal Development Seminar she attended, called the Life Success Course. Being a part of her Self-Discovery Process was an honor and privilege. I found her to be as real as it gets, right out of the gates. She is Authentic and Willing to be challenged and still work through the hard stuff to get to the good stuff.

We interacted again a few months later in August of 2013, when she attended the Women's Leadership Seminar. Once again, she showed up in true form of who she is. Let me say it this way, one will never have to question what Staci is ever thinking or feeling in a moment. It is expressed clearly.

Then a few months later, we got to be together again at an annual event for Leadership Graduates.

I was drawn to her from the start because we are both born and raised in Hawaii and we are both Japanese American Women. And what I love about her the most is her authenticity and willingness to say it like it is. There is no need for translation in a conversation with Staci. And underneath what could be perceived as a tough exterior, there is a woman with a big heart, a generous soul, and a real Visionary of assisting others in Living Their Life by Design.

One of our memorable moments together was when she was in it in a moment during the Life Success Course, and I say to her, "Being a tough Tita does NOT serve your right now! You are not walking down Kalakaua Avenue at 2 o'clock in the morning, so STOP IT!" She reminds me of this moment till today.

We have remained friends since. I have been with her in the struggle, in the joy, and in our shared love of Food. She has become my sister, my Ohana, as we say in Hawaii. She made a trip to Arizona from Hawaii to surprise me for my 50th birthday. And she continues to support me in living my own Vision with the same honesty and transparency since Day 1.

Staci is a successful business owner, and continuously works to sharpen her Leadership skills with her employees, her colleagues, as well as with the people in her personal life. Her ability to coach, guide, inspire and keep it real are gifts she offers to the people she chooses to interface with in both business and personal sectors of her life.

I say without a second thought that my life is blessed by having her in it. I continue to learn and grow in the hours of conversations we have together.

If you, too, want to learn, grow, and be inspired to Live Your Life by Design, contact Staci and strap yourself in for a Ride of Transformation.

Kareen Borzone

Author, Mentor, Trainer, Foodie and Friend

SECTION I

In this first section, we are going to explore both pigeonholes and Living Life by Design. You will find out what they both mean, how to identify and breakthrough pigeonholes, and how to design your own life.

CHAPTER 1

What Is Living Life by Design?

Most of us don't even design our own homes....

What is Living Life by Design? Living Life by Design is simply living life on your terms based on how you want to spend your time on this planet, including everything that entails. It means having the ability to go do whatever it is you want to do whenever you want, without the need for long-term planning, having to sacrifice anything, or dealing with grave repercussions afterward.

It starts with WHY. What's your driving force? Why do you get up and go to work? Why do you do the things that you do day in and day out? Why are you here? What is your greater purpose? Then, the WHAT. What is it that you truly love doing? What would you do if you could do anything? What would your life look like if you didn't have the stresses of everyday life that are put on you by society?

Looking at the whys in our life helps us to identify and prioritize what we really want. For example, a single parent of four may find out that their greatest WHY, are their children; they would do anything to take care of them. Everything they do, every decision they make, and how they live their own life may all be based on what they believe is best for their children.

In today's society, we are told how to live, what is acceptable, and who we are supposed to be. This is not true at all; we can get up every morning and live the life that we want to live, every single day. That is Living Life by Design.

CHAPTER 2

Are You Living Life by Design?

"Living you BEST life"
Isn't Living Life By Design

You may simply say, I'm working at "my dream job," or, "I'm living my best life." But, I challenge you with this: are you really? If you were to look at your life 24/7/365, are you completely ecstatic about what you are doing 100% of the time? The answer is probably a hard truth to face, but it's

NO! Now the next question is, why?

The answer to that question is a little more complex, and it can take many jabs of the shovel to dig up your specific answer to this question. However, it starts with settling.

Settling seems to be the biggest, broadest, most general way for us to sweep stuff under the "do we really want that" rug. We settle for the best-paying job that we "can get" to be able to provide for our own best life or the best lives of our families. We settle for seeing our loved ones on the weekend cause we're too busy trying to provide or make money. We settle for the "stay-cation" versus the trip to Italy. We settle for the life we have instead of the life that we want and deserve. And let me be the first to tell you, you deserve the life you want.

In our efforts to settle, one more way to sweep stuff under

the "do we really want that" rug pops up way too often. And that's when we say, "Someday! Someday…"

Someday we'll take that dream Alaskan cruise that we're always talking about. Someday we'll build the addition to the house, so we can have friends and family visit whenever they want. Someday we'll get that car we really want. In the Meantime, let's settle for this compact A series that is justifiably practical because of X, Y and Z.

Please don't misunderstand. I am not suggesting that you quit your job, drain your savings, sell everything that you have, and do whatever you want to do without responsibility or some sort of income. What I am suggesting, however, is to find something that you're passionate about and figure out how to create an income to sustain the lifestyle you choose to live—your Life by Design.

CHAPTER 3

What the Pigeon?

Pigeonholes: What? How? Why? Huh?

Pigeonholes, labels, programs—it's all the same when it comes down to it. We allow others to put labels on us, justify circumstances and accept our mediocre state because of these universal understandings of who or why we are the way we are. You could even go as far as saying that pigeonholes allow themselves to be used as an excuse or reason someone is or isn't something, has or doesn't have something, or are capable or not of doing something.

Pigeonholes are labels, limiting beliefs, programs, and excuses that have been put on you by someone or something else. Most of the time, pigeonholes are created by and put on you by people who are close to you and spend enough time with you to "know" who you are and what you are all about Sometimes, though rarely, are they put on you by strangers that you have only one interaction with.

Pigeonholes are simply created based off a situation, a preexisting condition, or a term that is often out of your control. They can come from anyone at any time, and they are sometimes created and put on you to make the other person more comfortable with the current situation.

As children, we get a lot of limiting beliefs and pigeonholes put on us. We get classified in the first few years of school. You're either "smart" or not, "talented" or not, "skilled in a sport" or not, "musical," "artistic," "innovative" or not.

Our teachers do it: "Little Johnny has great potential, if only he would apply himself." Parents do it: "My son is so good at soccer, but he won't be able to pay the bills with that skill." Even our peers do it: "You don't have this, aren't capable of that, or won't ever be what you want, because of A, B, or C."

Pigeonholes are not always easy to identify. However, if there are things that you believe you really want that you don't have, the "reason," "excuse," or "justification" that prevents you from having it is your pigeonhole. It could be as specific as a medical condition or as broad as being lazy.

CHAPTER 4

Ka-Pow! Take That!

Drop-Kick That Sh!t! Breaking Through Those Pesky Pigeonholes

Breaking through a pigeonhole is simple in concept, but it can be extremely difficult in actuality. First, you need to identify the pigeonholes, and then make a conscious decision and take daily action to become who you want to be to best serve the life you want.

Without breaking through the pigeonholes that have limited you, you will be stuck living your life by society's or someone else's design. Have you ever felt that you could not do something that you really wanted to do? And because of that feeling of "could not," you did not? Well, the reason why you did not do it was probably because there was a pigeonhole that was put on you at some point in your life that you believed to be true, or maybe you simply accepted it.

Now you may be asking yourself, "Why break through these pigeonholes?" Well, if you haven't figured that out yet, let me tell you: it's to get to where you want to be. These pesky things are what have been and are currently holding you back from the things you really want and from being able to spend your time doing things that truly set your soul ablaze, and all with the people you choose to be beside of you, not the crap storm of people you are forced to tolerate on a regular basis because you "work with them."

Breaking through pigeonholes is very important; otherwise, they kind of define your life and then your entire existence orbits around them. Like a dog on a chain tied to a spike in the ground, you are only able to go as far as the chain allows. You are limited by that chain, and you will never get any further than the limits of that chain unless you are able to break that chain or work it free.

You get up every day, Monday through Friday, go to your job, and do your thing. There's nothing really exciting. You may be working towards goals for a promotion at work. These goals have been defined by your boss to get a promotion you may or may not want. If you don't want it, you have adopted your boss's belief that you want it, and yet you don't truly own it.

So until you break through these pigeonholes and the things that are holding you back, you will never be able to live the life you really want, whatever that looks like.

Wouldn't it be amazing to be able to choose every component of every moment   of your life? Don't get to technical and argue that you can't control the weather, because if you decide to go to Arizona knowing they are expecting a monsoon but you plan to enjoy the sunny, dry desert atmosphere, then that's all on you. You can't expect the heavens to part and the sun to come beaming down the moment your plane touches down on the tarmac at Sky Harbor Airport. So, get your head out of the clouds and let's land on your little piece of heaven here on earth.

The other thing that you can't control is how other people react or respond to certain situations. There is good news here though: you can control your circle and who you allow into your world. If you know your friend Sally doesn't like the sun and sand and that she will probably complain the whole time until you surrender to leaving, Sally may not be the friend you want to hang out with at the beach. Instead, she may be the person you want to do something indoors with. You can also control what affects you and what you focus on. Even if you do decide that you want to hang out with Sally at the beach, and she agrees to go, you could focus on the crystal blue water, the gorgeous clear sky, and the people around you enjoying themselves, instead of your miserable friend dusting sand off her towel. (I do recommend taking separate cars.)

Let me ask you this? What would your ideal day look like? Think about every component of that day. Who you're with, what you're doing, where you are, and what you hear, smell, taste, see, etc. Now, think about how you would make this happen in your current situation. What planning and arrangements would need to take place? How much lead time would everyone involved need? What would need to change in order for you to have your ideal day with everyone you said would be involved? If you're now thinking, "Well, that's impossible!" You're absolutely right; based on your pigeonholes, it is impossible. However, without the pigeonholes that hold you back, everything and anything you desire is VERY POSSIBLE!

Take it a step further and you will be able to design your life DAILY! Imagine being able to take a day trip to another place and time on a moment's notice. Fly into town to have dinner with a friend who called and is having a rough time. Jet set to a foreign country because it's beautiful this time of year and you want to experience it. Get up every morning at 4:30 to walk your dogs and spend time with them, because they are your world and you can. Or simply sit down to two meals a day with your kids because you're not rushing off to work or focused on other day-to-day stuff.

What if you were able to wake up EVERY SINGLE DAY and feel excited to be alive, living life full out, playing the biggest game you could possible play, and doing it all wherever you wanted to on the planet? That's what Living Life by Design looks like for you. No one else can be the architect of your life; only you can hold the pencil and draft its true vision.

CHAPTER 5

There's NOT ENOUGH Time!

When did my daughter turn 21!?! Where did the time go!?!

I can't tell you how many parents I've worked with have said things like, "I don't know where the time has gone!" or, "It seems like just yesterday I was changing little Brandon's diapers, and he just got his driver's license last week!"

Think about it: time is the only thing we cannot get back. Time is the one thing that we take for granted, until we lose a loved one or miss a "once in a lifetime opportunity", we don't really think about it. When members of our family we were once close to, or a friend we used to spend every day with when life was "simpler" passes away, we are immediately forced to deal with our own demise. We automatically start thinking about time and how precious it truly is. Now, if we're being honest, that feeling doesn't last long, and before we know it, we are back into the hustle and bustle of our everyday lives.

Even when missing that "once in a lifetime opportunity", we dwell on the "what ifs" of the situation. What if we did it? What if we could do it? Blah, blah, blah. Well, if you passed up that "once in a lifetime opportunity", it's gone forever, or maybe if you're lucky enough, it goes into your "someday" bucket.

Even with deadlines for school, work, or taxes, we tend to default to "there's always tomorrow" or "I'll do it later." But the reality is, there is only one today, there is only now and nothing else exists. God willing you don't, however, you could be hit by a bus this afternoon and never be able to get to "tomorrow" or that "later" that you are such a fan of.

Can you imagine if you leveraged the now instead of putting it off until the later? If you plotted out your schedule to include all the heavy lifting of a project at the beginning so you had time to tweak the last minute changes and still feel comfortable and confident that you produced the best result all the time. Or heaven forbid, you complete a project early and under promise and over deliver. These wouldn't be the worst things to be known for, and I am positive your stress levels will go down.

Why wouldn't you want your stress levels to go down? Why wouldn't you want to start Living Life by Design immediately? Well, the answer is simply: pigeonholes. Something, somewhere within you, is frantically yelling,

"STOP! YOU CAN'T DO THAT!" Then comes the pigeonhole: "You need to stay in your high stress, mediocre paying job to continue to make what you need to pay the babysitter, the mortgage, and everything that you say you need. You need to maintain the cushy little lifestyle for you and your family, but without your mediocre pay, you won't be able to." Blah, blah, blah. My all-time favorite pigeonhole that most of us carry around in some form at some point in our lives is, "WHO THE HELL DO YOU THINK YOU ARE!?! No one is going to want to hear what you have to say!" Blah, blah, blah.

What if you were to muffle the noise? Stop the frantic yelling. One of the tools that I use whenever someone or something inside me is telling me that I can't, is Charlie Brown's teacher. As soon as I hear the judgment, criticism, or pigeonholes come up, I tune out until all I hear is useless, unidentifiable sounds, because that is what it truly is.

It is fact that successful people are masters of one thing, and that is time. If this is true, and time is the one thing we can never get back, then why waste it on the pigeonholes and the nay-sayers? Focus your time on becoming the best version of yourself to be able to truly Live Life by Design.

SECTION II

In this section, I am going to expose my most vulnerable pigeonholes. I am doing this to provide examples of how they come to be, how they can and will continue to pop up if you allow them to, and what I did or am doing to breakthrough.

Trust me when I say, this book has reset the spark to a lot of my personal pigeonholes and created more opportunities to sharpen my breakthrough tools and move forward.

CHAPTER 6

Stop That Dog!

What the Hell Just Happened?

When I was 13 months old, I was playing on the floor in the living room/kitchen area. The family pet was also in the same area. My mother was busy in the kitchen and could not have anticipated what would happen next.

The family pet, a beloved pit bull companion that was a part of the family before my birth, couldn't fully comprehend what was going on. It was the first time I, the tertiary family member, was outside of my space. I didn't have a visual boundary or set limitations to "my space" on the floor, which translated to now being in "his space." Knowing now what I know about dogs, I was seen as a threat. So, he did what any animal would do when a threat is posed, and he attacked without warning. He picked me up by the top of the head, and being the breed that he was, he locked his jaw around my skull. He then proceeded to toss me around like a rag doll.

My mother shocked and in disbelief was able to navigate the situation as best as she could. She grabbed a metal serving tray, probably the one from my highchair, this was the 70s after all, and started hitting the animal that she loved so much on top of his head. More shocked than probably hurt, the dog released its death grip and my mom picked me up off the floor. She wrapped my head in whatever towels she could find, and seeing that my father had the only family vehicle at work, she started walking the mile or so down the old dirt road and out of the gulch that we lived in. Luckily for both of us, a neighbor was in his field tending to it.

He immediately turned his attention from his field that he was tending to, to   my mother when he heard my mother's screaming for help. Upon realizing what was going on, he jumped into his truck and picked us up. My mother was unable to make contact with my father at work, so she asked her sister to keep trying. While driving out of the gulch, we met my father, whom my aunt had successfully contacted and was racing home.

At the emergency room, the doctors, nurses, and staff didn't know what to make of the situation and decided my best chance at survival was to have me airlifted to the children's hospital that may be better equipped to handle the situation. My parents were instructed to meet me there via their personal vehicle. While I was being transported via helicopter to the children's hospital some 20+ miles away, my parents drove. Needless to say, they beat the helicopter to the children's hospital, and of course panic struck!

After what seemed like an eternity, I finally arrived. The doctors immediately started assessing the situation and my condition, and they came to two possible conclusions. First, is that I wouldn't survive. Seeing that I had lost a lot of blood, not to mention brain matter and probably spinal fluid, there was little chance that anyone could survive this successfully, let alone a child this young. There had been too much trauma. And even if I did survive this, the second option, in my opinion, was more awful than death. The doctors told my grief-stricken parents that I would end up paralyzed on my right side and have little to no brain function. Basically, I would be a vegetable, and who the hell would want that?

Obviously, it affected me and my parents greatly. The entire future of my existence had shifted from a "promising future" most toddlers have to "if I were to survive this, then what?" My future wasn't as promising as it had been just hours before.

The doctors started cleaning the injuries the best they could. In order to do so, they had to do additional cutting of my scalp.

Seeing as it was the best way possible, they decided to cut from ear to ear over the top of my head, pull the skin back, and do the best they could to clean the wound and stitch it all back up. There was concern about brain function, mobility, speech—all of it.

As time went on, I started to get better. As a toddler, not really comprehending what role people played in my life, I was more excited to see one particular nurse than my own mother. This particular nurse tended to my every need, and my mother seemed like a stranger who would come and visit. It broke my mother's heart.

My mother would sit in the hospital garden and rub her worries into a small rock that fit perfectly into her hand, praying to God the whole time that I would make it and in some miraculous way that I'd be "okay." My father found himself negotiating with an entity he didn't even believe existed. He bargained with God, telling Him that if He were to save his little girl, he would give up fighting chickens (something that he was extremely passionate about, and was long before my existence). I don't know if it was my mother's "worry rock" or the "bargaining my father did with his new-found God" that was the tipping point, however for some reason, I survived. I spent just a few short weeks in the hospital and without medical explanation, I was released as a healthier version of what was expected. Cognitively, I could expect deficiencies, physically, there would be some shortcomings for sure, and I would probably suffer from seizures the rest of my short expected life.

This was the first, and probably the most impactful, pigeonhole that I have been put in, and it is what I now refer to as "The Dog Bite."

CHAPTER 7

It Was a Normal Childhood

Or so I Thought....

I had a fairly "normal" childhood, or so I thought. I went to a private school from preschool through intermediate, and I was a mediocre student. I played sports, like a sloth, but I was on the teams that I wanted to be on. I was forced, due to curriculum design, to try my hand at choir, hand bells, and even band.

I went to a public high school and did the loner thing. I barely passed my freshmen year, hated life, and just showed up as much as I could tolerate the last three years and graduated (on time!).

I moved on to college, working part-time while doing so, paying my own way. It took me 4.5 years, to get my two-year degree in Liberal Arts, but more importantly, it took that long to figure out school wasn't for me.

This is what my life looked like when strangers looked in. However, for years, I saw neurologists, speech therapists, and other medical professionals. Looking back on it, I think my parents were waiting for the rug to get pulled out from under them. They were waiting for some doctor to put a hard and fast time frame on my life. But to me, it was just something that I did, and I thought, "Yup, everybody's doing it." I didn't think that seeing "specialty doctors" or "therapists" was a big deal. But obviously everyone else did not, and it was kind of a big deal.

All my shortcomings, my weight issues, my speech clarity, my laziness, my grades, my depression, and anything else that I fell short at or failed in were all justified in my mother's eyes, especially by this one event. "The Dog Bite" was the excuse for everything that I was not; it was the yardstick that I was measured up against.

Please understand that by the time I realized that this pigeonhole existed, my father was absent most of the time; working 18+ hour days, 6-7 days a week to help secure my current and future financial stability. I remember my father telling me throughout my life, "Kid, you can go flip burgers for the rest of your life and still travel two times a year. You're set; you won't have to worry."

Reflecting on this now, this was probably his way of overcompensating for what had happened to me so very long ago.

It wasn't until high school that I started to notice that this running theme for all my failures and shortcomings was exactly the same thing. And so I decided that it was no longer going to be part of my story. Prior to that point, everyone in my life knew about "The Dog Bite," as if it were a part of my name. I often thought that introductions, especially from my mother, may have gone something like, "This is my daughter Staci. She was bitten in the head by a dog when she was 13 months old and almost died. So... (*insert necessary excuse, justification or cautionary tale here)." It was the reputation that proceeded me, whether I wanted it to or not. But from then on, that story was told by choice, not by chance. I started looking at who I was without this pigeonhole. It was hard to do, because I didn't know what that even looked like.

CHAPTER 8

It Wasn't Such a BAD Life

Despite "The Dog Bite"....

I have held jobs and had careers in childcare, education, business management, office management, sales, and marketing. I have started and failed at business multiple times.

When I graduated from high school, I got my first job with a large non-profit community organization. I stayed there, working my way through their different programs in aquatics, childcare, and sports. I even volunteered with their teen programs as a mentor and chaperone.

Four and a half years later, I moved into retail briefly, then found myself working for the largest private education entity there was, in a job that I was heavily underqualified for.

Up until that point in my life, I probably did the most growth into who I really was meant to be. Being a barely 20-something-year-old, at my first full-time job and on a team that was at average 20+ years my senior, supported that growth tremendously. I also found my passions for teaching and learning. Not just my own learning, but how others learn, types of learners, and how to successfully teach the same lessons to different types of learners at the same time.

This started the journey that I am on now. In those short four and a half years, a fire started in me that has been burning ever since without me ever realizing it.

After being with that group, I moved on to my dream job: BARISTA! That's right! I was a BARISTA! Woo-hoo! It was a fun place to work, I met a lot of really interesting people, and for the first time ever, I was the senior being supervised by kids 10+ years my junior.

I like to look at these short years of my life as my midlife crisis. Granted, I was in my late 20s and even transitioned to my 30s while there, but in hindsight, I was hanging on to my youth and doing so while my age-appropriate peers were starting their careers.

It was fun while it lasted, and I had worked my way up the coffee shop mountain to as highs as I wanted, so it was time to move on. I found myself in an office cubicle making copies and running inter-office mail from office to office, all while the older woman on the other side of the cubicle wall bought her time to retirement by making phone calls about her grandchildren and slipping into one of her multiple naps every day. I couldn't take it! It obviously didn't last long, and I moved on.

I found myself in another office cubicle making copies, filing documents, and running inter-office mail from building to building. It must have been a step up because I got to see sunlight during the day and the woman sitting on the other side of the cubicle wall spent most of her time reading the latest novels from her favorite authors. At least there, I knew I didn't have to silently slink past her space for fear of waking her up. Though the job was easy, the pay was decent,   and I even moved myself up the office structured corporate ladder. I hated the politics and the bullsh!t that came with it and eventually despised going to work.

Even though I had tried and failed at business several times before, probably because of lack of experience, commitment, and willingness to let go of anything within it, I thought this was it! The time was now! So, I quit that awful political cesspool of an office, sold the house that I was living in (and had just bought 11 months prior) for seed money, and moved back in with my mother. I was an only child and single. We had just lost my father several years prior, and she was living alone in a 3-bedroom house with my dogs, so it made sense. I did keep my investment property in tack for continuous income and collateral in case I needed it.

Now, I am currently celebrating our 7th anniversary of a small food service business in Hawai'i. I've started another business with a target launch date in just   a few months, and I still have my investment property. I also travel any time I desire, create my own schedule, and Live Life by Design. Not bad for "The Dog Bite" girl, huh!?!

I have dealt with "The Dog Bite" pigeonhole all my life, and it still comes up today. Just the other week, while casually talking about my latest bout of depression, my mother said, "You know, you may be depressed because of the dog bite..." She continued to support her theory by talking about a "guy" she knows who had a bad concussion decades ago and has developed depression just recently. I simply turned to look at her and said, "You're still using this as an excuse. Wow!"

Whenever "The Dog Bite" pigeonhole comes up, or when I find myself struggling with this excuse, I take a minute to identify it. I look at it and make a conscious decision to continue on with who I am and what I am doing.

CHAPTER 9

What!?! Another One!?!

Wasn't "The Dog Bite" Enough...

I have always struggled with my weight. My earliest school-day photos show me as pudgy, fat, whatever. I even resembled the Michelin Tire Man with rolls in my forearms. However, I didn't see it as "that big of a deal." Both my parents were overweight, and I was still "allowed" to participate in whatever sports activities I wanted to be in, both in and out of school.

Looking back as to why I was overweight, it wasn't a mystery. My father had programs and behaviors ingrained in him around food growing up. His parents and grandparents would ration his portions to prevent him from overeating, even though he was still hungry and an athlete in high school. I remember him telling me that he would have to sneak his snacks so he wouldn't get into trouble. My mother had similar experiences with food scarcity being one of four sisters growing up in the household. Having lived through the Great Depression and having the scarcity mentality instilled in my grandparents, they passed on that behavior to my both my parents respectively.

My parents, doing what parents do, didn't want me going through what they did, so my food intake wasn't monitored, and I was provided with anything that I desired. Not being the most agile, athletic child, I wasn't nearly as active as I should have been, especially eating what I was eating.

I wasn't really aware that I WAS FAT until my eighth grade teacher held me back afterschool to talk to me. As if that wasn't publicly embarrassing enough, he had the bus driver hold the bus until he was "finished talking to me." I have blocked out the details of the conversation. However, I do remember him telling me that he was "concerned" about my size, and he wanted to "help" me by having me walk laps before school, during PE, and after school when possible. I also remember that we were having this conversation as he was casually sipping on a can of Hawaiian Sun juice that he had gotten out of the student vending machine. Though his intentions may have been honorable, I found the experience to be condescending and demoralizing. This was the start of my next pigeonhole called, "I'm FAT."

From that moment, I wasn't only sitting in the world of "you're not good enough or smart enough, and your speech is funny, etc." but now I WAS FAT TOO! My already low self-esteem hit rock bottom. I started to become more aware of my presence, the amount of space I took up, etc.

By the time I was a senior in high school, with food as my only consistent comfort and friend, I was tipping the scale at around 330 lbs. The only reason I don't have a specific weight, is because the dial on the scale at my house maxed out at the 330-lb. mark.

Of course, it didn't help that food was the primary love language growing up, due to my parent's own programs around food.

CHAPTER 10

You're MORE THAN "Just FAT"

*What the F*ck is "MORBIDLY OBESE"!?!*

My weight has come up with several individuals time and time again throughout my lifetime.

My aunt attempted to support my weight loss by "rewarding," aka "bribing," me with money for every pound I lost within a period of time that she set. Though her intentions may have been good, this just fed my programs of not being good enough. The downfall to her process was that money was not motivating to me. In the world that I lived in, being an only child and the only grandchild on my father's side, money was never a motivating factor.

When I was 21, I had to go in for a physical for a specialized drivers' license. I had to go see the physician chosen by my employer at the time to get my medical clearance. I already knew that I was "FAT," but the health report stated otherwise. I will never forget seeing "MORBIDLY OBESE" handwritten under "Other Health Concerns." I remember being confused, hurt, and ashamed.

It was the first time I had ever seen that term. I knew that I was heavy. I knew that I was a cow or whatever else people were calling me. I knew all of that, but for whatever reason, seeing "MORBIDLY OBESE" written on a piece of paper was super impactful. I'm not sure if it was because of the language that was being used or the situation in which I had to get this done. But for whatever reason, it stuck. I also didn't turn in the physical report out of embarrassment. I didn't understand or even knew the intensity of the situation or the seriousness of the situation until I had to go in for a physical to get this specialized drivers' license.

Then, when I was asked to be a part of some bridal parties, I declined whenever possible, not because I didn't want to, but because I didn't want the bridal party to have to be put through such a torturous ordeal of having to find a dress. And when I felt like I had to commit to participating in a bridal party, they would have to have the dresses custom-made because I couldn't buy off the rack, and don't get me started on shoes.

Getting the dresses made was problem number 1; finding a dress that I was okay with was problem number 2. Having fit friends who looked good in practically anything, and wanting to find something that they could use again, was a problem. So I just surrendered and settled for whatever it was that they wanted regardless of how I looked or felt.

But as crushing as those were for me, nothing was more demeaning then when   I graduated high school and applied to be a summer fun group leader with an organization that I practically grew up in as a child and had dedicated all my free time to from the moment I started 7th grade to the receiving of my high school diploma. Seeing as I was such a committed and dedicated individual to this nonprofit organization, they saw this as a teachable moment. I remember going into my "interview" and finding out that I would not be selected to be a group leader. However, they did have a plan for me. As I sat there nervously anticipating what was about to happen, I remember feeling my programs of not being good enough flare up. What I didn't realize at the time was that I was about to get the most intense boost I have ever had to my "I'm FAT" pigeonhole.

I sat there in gratitude as they delivered the plan. I was so committed to this organization that I, at the time, obviously was blinded by their abuse and mistreatment of my individual situation. My soon-to-be "supervisor," the aquatics director, said "You're not quite 'ready' to be a group leader yet. But if you are willing to work in our aquatics department and teach swimming this summer, you will be 'ready' for the school year." I will never forget what she said next, "If someone like YOU can walk around in a swimsuit all summer..." Yup, I stopped listening. Knowing that I had a paying position was enough for me, and I settled.

Now, here are the facts that add insult to the very traumatic conversation that I had just had. Facts, mind you that they didn't look into, or didn't care about if they had. First, I could barely swim. Remember, I wasn't athletic at all growing up, and it took me years to realize that I had the ability to float. Second, there was no training, instruction, or direction as to how to teach swimming, technique, etc. Third, I was left to my own devices to teach my own class with a student volunteer, if the class were big enough. And fourth, and the most important fact, they were putting their students at risk. Even with the proper floatation devices on, a child can still drown.

I did that "job" for over a year and earned my position as a group leader the school year immediately following my senior year of high school. But I didn't learn anything really, except that aquatics was not my thing.

It wasn't until years later that I realized that I was a joke. I was something to mock and make fun of. Something to use as a "role model" when kids were self-conscious about their bodies. And in hindsight, the only thing I can say that was positive about this experience was my tan at the time. Looking back at it now, all I know is that was the most pivotal point for me and my "I'm FAT" pigeonhole.

CHAPTER 11

F*ck That Sh!t!

I'm done with being "MORBIDLY OBESE" or even "FAT" for that matter...

It wasn't until after college that I started becoming somewhat conscious about the causes and effects of diet and exercise and calories in versus energy out.

Without any real effort, additional movement, or change in diet, I started to "lose weight." By the time I was out of college, I was around 250 lbs. I didn't know exact numbers because the scale was something I would only see at the doctor's office.

Being "comfortable" at around 250 lb, a friend wanted me to go with him to the gym. He was a fit, athletic guy who was starting to feel the results of "getting older" (mind you, we were still in our early 20s). I hired a trainer and just went with the flow. I lost about 50 lbs with her until she moved a little over a year later, then picked up about 20. I remember thinking "220? I can live with 220." And then life caught up with me: diabetes and joint issues started.

In my early 30s, I was approached by a "classmate" from high school (whom I didn't think knew my name then, so I was shocked she did almost 15 years later), about a networking marketing "opportunity." The product, a new and "upcoming" all natural energy drink, was making claims of weight loss and extreme health improvement. Being what I now know as an extroverted-introvert, I jumped on.

During my somewhat miserable 3 years with this group, they created all kinds of marketing and promo gimmicks and challenges. One in particular was the "High School Weight Challenge." It was a 30- or 90-day challenge, depending on your "level of commitment (to yourself)" where the participants would attempt to get back to the weight they were in high school. Now, most of the participants were well into their 30s or older, so to push back the scale that far was nearly impossible. During the challenge, participants were to publicly shame themselves for motivation by drinking 3 product drinks a day and measure and weigh themselves on camera to be posted, shared, and used as marketing on social media and other networking platforms.

Seeing as I already weighed less than I did in high school, I changed the challenge slightly to the "Half My High School Weight Challenge." Most of the participants didn't see the results they were after, were forced to buy three times the required auto-ship, and drove up sales with empty promises. All of this was the result of a brilliant marketing idea and because one guy lost weight while using the product, so they made up some program formula for the masses. This was my first real attempt at stopping the "I'm FAT" pigeonhole. Not only did I fail at this attempt, but the whole experience with this group fed all my programs of not being enough!

After that fiasco, I started feeling sluggish and tired all the time, and I just wanted to eat fatty, greasy, or sugary foods and lay on the couch. Surprisingly, my weight didn't teeter too much, and I stayed in the 220-230 range for most of my 30s.

By the end of my 30s, I was closer to 200. Don't ask me how or why; I just was. But my health was getting worse. In my 20s, I was diagnosed with Type 2 diabetes, which I just accepted as hereditary. But in my 30s alone, I suffered from pneumonia, had a crucial bout of cellulitis, and started suffering from migraines and joint pain. I was even "diagnosed" with arthritis, bursitis, and tendinitis in both lower extremities in the ankles, knees, and hips respectively by a therapist.

So, I started to focus more energy on what my diet looked like and how I was burning those calories. I needed to go through these struggles over and over again for me to get to where I wanted to be as an end result.

Now in my forties, residual back and hip pain started from carrying all the excess weight when I was younger. And just 5 months ago, after months of inconclusive testing, I had a stent placed in the front vessel of my heart. When I went to my internist with jaw pain and chest discomfort, he did an EKG and it seemed "okay." However, being concerned about the pain, he referred me to a cardiologist. The cardiologist referred to my internist's EKG results and scheduled a treadmill stress test. After the results of that came back inconclusive, despite the jaw pain occurring during the test, he decided to do a nuclear stress test. The pictures taken during this test showed something, but it wasn't clear as to its severity. However, again with the jaw pain occurring during the treadmill portion of the test, he recommended a cardiac catheterization procedure, which helped him discover the problem.

Apparently, there were two blockages. The first was a 100% blockage in the back vessel. This apparently had bi-passed itself because I was working out so much. I am told that I had pushed my heart to its limit, and instead of failing, the blood flow was able to create another vessel to provide that portion of the heart with the blood supply it needed. It was the second blockage in the front vessel that needed the stent. It was at 99% blockage and cause for concern. The cardiologist put in a stent, and I have been on the mend regarding this since.

Even as I sit and write this, I have a skin infection on my

chest and a tail bone contusion. But I'm still going, working, more driven and determined than ever.

Every single time I am faced with a health issue, or every time I decide to put something in my mouth, I think of the possible repercussions and adjust accordingly. I weigh myself and test my blood glucose level daily, and I am currently at the lightest weight I have been since intermediate school. My glucose levels are still high and my vision has gotten worse because of it, but I am not stopping. Most, if not all with enough digging, of my health ailments and conditions are related to my "I'm FAT" pigeonhole. I accepted it for too long and allowed it to cause too much damage. I may not be exactly where I wanted to be by now, but I am working with a dedicated team of professionals, both medically and fitness-related, to get me where I want to be.

I may still be heavier than my "ideal weight," I may be bigger than I would like to be, and I may never fit into a size 6, but I am done with owning and identifying with the "I'm FAT" pigeonhole.

SECTION III

This last Section will take you through a brief introduction to the necessary steps and provide tools and techniques for you to Design your Life.

CHAPTER 12

It's Time to Design Your Life

My Eight D Approach to Life by Design:
What are they and how to use them...

While coaching people on how to design their life, I refer to my Eight D Approach to Living Life by Design.

I developed the Eight D Approach to Life by Design to simplify the design process. We all struggle at times with what we think we want, or even maybe what we are told we should want, for ourselves and by extension for our families.

Because of this, I have broken down the complex design process into six more manageable steps. There are no limits or formulas as to how long each step should take. However, the steps should be completed and identified in the order in which they are presented for maximum and complete effectiveness.

If you do decide, for whatever reason, to do it "your way," please understand that at some point in your process, you will have to circle around to all the Seven Ds in order to effectively complete the Eighth D. So why not make it easier on yourself and just trust the process as it is provided for you below.

May I also suggest, that because the Eighth D is always changing and evolving with your life, that you consolidate all your note-taking on this approach to separate notebooks, a working Word document, etc. that is specifically for this process.

Now, let's get started.

The first D stands for DEFINE. You may think that DEFINING who you are may be easy. However, if you truly dig deep into who you are and get completely honest, raw, and real, you will find that it is not easy. You will need to take time on this first D. It really starts with identifying the pigeonholes that have been holding you back, breaking through these pigeonholes consciously, and moving forward. It may even cause you to own something completely new and to change from who you thought you were to who you really are.

The second D stands for DECIDE. This is the time for you to DECIDE who you want to be, now that you have defined who you are. DECIDE how you want to live your life. DECIDE for yourself what it is you want your life to look like.

The third D stands for DESTROY! Yes, it's time to DESTROY those things that you no longer want in your life. Now that you have defined who you are and decided what you want your life to look like, there are things in your life that no longer serve you. Take the time to DESTORY those things and breakthrough the pigeonholes that you have discovered in the process.

The fourth D stands for DESIRE. Although, it takes some thought, ask yourself what you DESIRE and why. It may be the specific boat that you want, because it is similar to the boat you had as a child—the one you spent a lot of time on with your grandfather who has since passed away. Or it may be being able to take your children to your favorite place on the planet, because it is so special to you and you want to share the stories and the joy with them. Whatever it is you want, make sure that the why you want it is important. I am a strong believer in this belief: if your whys are great enough, the how will appear. If you give up before getting what you want, or if you settle for anything less, you may need to reevaluate your why.

The fifth D stands for DRIVE. DRIVE simply means making conscious decisions to live life however it is you want to live it. The tricky part of this, is making those conscious decisions, even when it's not the easiest or most convenient time to do it. DRIVE will point you in the right direction when things get off track. DRIVE can be called upon by asking yourself if what you are currently doing is in alignment with what you DESIRE.

The sixth D stands for DEDICATION. DEDICATION will keep you committed to your wants. DEDICATION will overcome the doubts and the inconveniences. DECIDATION will help you clear away the cobwebs of distractions that may try to get in your way, both from yourself and from outside entities.

The seventh D stands for DETERMINATION. DETERMINATION will keep your wants, your goals, your dreams, and your desires at the forefront of your mind. Though it may seem very similar to DRIVE, this could not be further from the truth. DETERMINATION allows you space to work your DESIRES and to find new ways to get from where you are to where you want to be. It feeds the never-give-up fire within you when it shows signs of it possibly beginning to smolder out.

The eighth and final D stands for DESIGN. DESIGN is temporary; it is always evolving as you evolve. It is never your end-all be-all, and it will change over time. Your DESIGN may look completely different from day to day, and it is up to you to decide what it looks like. DESIGN is the goals that you want for your life. These are the things you get to do, instead of have to do.

CHAPTER 13

So, What Is It Really?

What is Living Life by Design....?

No one else can tell you what Living Life by Design looks like. It is all individualized to you and your wants, needs, and desires. You DEFINE who you are, you DECIDE what your life will look like moving forward, and DESTROY what is standing in your way and those pesky pigeonholes. Take a look at what it is you DESIRE, and it is your DRIVE, DEDICATION, and DETERMINATION that allow you to DESIGN your life.

Get rid of the pigeonholes that were placed upon you. If it helps, write them down on individual pieces of paper, and one by one, set them on fire, tear them into bit-size pieces, or destroy them in some way.

Get comfortable with who you are, accept where you are in life, and decide where you want to go. Put your unwavering stake in the ground for yourself, stand strong, and own your greatness. The fact is, you deserve to Live the Life that YOU Design. So, go ahead and get started. Your life is waiting for you!

CHAPTER 14

But I Still Don't Feel Comfortable

I want to do this, but I'm scared....

If ever you feel defeated, deflated, or just want to give up, look to your support system, whomever they may be. Reach out to them. I recommend calling or texting them to get their immediate attention and "borrow" their belief in you. Explain to them that your pigeonholes are flaring up and that you need their support.

Tell them you need to "borrow" their beliefs in you, and ask them for a list of 10-15 reasons why they believe you deserve whatever it is you desire. Now, sit back and allow them to give you the accolades you deserve! If it helps, call a few friends or family members and repeat this process.

You can even jot some of these down on little slips of paper with their names and dates on them and keep the collection individually folded in a jar or box. That way, if you cannot reach a member of your support system right away, you'll have that resource to tap into.

And if nothing else, know that I believe you deserve to LIVE your LIFE by your DESIGN!

About the Author

Who is Staci A. Imamura?

Staci A. Imamura was born and raised in Hawai`i. She still resides there where she shares a home with her mother and, despite "the dog bite," her two large male Rottweilers.

She currently is a business owner of two businesses. The first is a food service business, where she shares her passion for both food and being of service. The second is a life coaching business where she and her team provide compassionate and motivating coaching and education to create opportunities for their clients to Live Life by Design.

Besides being an owner of multiple businesses, Staci is a philanthropist, author, and coach. She is a property investor and is driven and passionate about assisting others to Live Life By their own Design.

Staci is a proud life-long learner and has been a student of Bob Proctor, Tony Robbins, Dave Ramsey, Brian Tracy, Dr. Wayne W. Dyer and PSI Seminars to name just a few.

Staci is a self-proclaimed coffee connoisseur and foodie. She enjoys traveling, is an avid reader and loves to cook. She is always striving to be bigger, better and different. She truly believes that in order to be the best in anything you first have to be the best version of yourself.

For more information about Staci Imamura's coaching programs, future books, events and other tools please visit: www.teachablemomentscoaching.com.

You can also follow Staci on Facebook at Staci Imamura, Author or on Instagram @staci.imamura for information on all of her latest projects and programs!